MW01291566

Also By Pamela D. Garcy, Ph.D.

The Power of Inner Guidance
The REBT Super-Activity Guide

Chapter contributions in:
Wake Up Moments of Inspiration
101 Great Ways To Enhance Your Career

How To Make Time When You Don't Have Any:

A New Approach To Reclaiming Your Schedule!

Pamela D. Garcy, Ph.D.

How To Make Time When You Don't Have Any:
A New Approach To Reclaiming Your Schedule!
by Pamela D. Garcy, Ph.D.

All rights reserved. No part of this book may be used
or reproduced by any means, graphic, electronic, or
mechanical, including photocopying, recording,
taping or by any information storage retrieval system
without the written permission of the author except in
the case of brief quotations embodied in
critical articles and reviews.

Copyright © 2010 by Pamela D. Garcy, Ph.D.
This book may be ordered by contacting
Pamela D. Garcy, Ph.D. at www.myinnerguide.com

Because of the dynamic nature of the Internet, any
Web addresses or links contained in this book may
have changed since publication
and may no longer be valid.

ISBN: 1453770186, EAN-13: 9781453770184.
Printed in the United States of America

Disclaimer: The information, ideas, and suggestions
in this book are not intended as a substitute for
professional advice. Before following any
suggestions contained in this book, you should
consult your personal physician or mental health
professional. The author shall not be liable or
responsible for any loss or damage allegedly arising
as a consequence of your use or application of any
information or suggestions in this book.
Author's note: Certain names and identifying
details have been changed to protect the
confidentiality of those mentioned in this book.

To My Favorite Time Travelers: Roger, Brittany, Ethan, And Max

Table of Contents

Acknowledgements

Thank you, Roger, my love and soul mate, for everything—especially for understanding when I came to bed so late during that week in September so I could finish writing. You are the most supportive husband out there, I'm sure.

Brittany, Ethan and Max, thank you for asking me when I was going to write another book! Thanks for understanding when I kicked you off of the computer. Also thanks for being a little bit quieter tonight so I could finish the manuscript.

Josh Cormie, thank you yet again for another outstanding book cover! I'm so lucky to have your creative brilliance on my team! It was fun playing with photos that day. I am very grateful & hope you'll help me fill up the shelf with more!

Thank you to everyone at WRJ who volunteered their time challenges. Also, thanks to Renee Roth for inviting me to speak and stimulating me to take this thought process to another level.

To my mastermind sisters Ellen, Sylvia, and Crystal, thank you for continuing to help me to "figure it all out." I cherish our weekly

i

calls and continue to be impressed with the manner in which each of you conducts your lives. You are wonderful and cherished. Thanks to Jack Canfield for bringing us together and for helping us to grow! We will see you in 2012 or sooner!

Thanks to my dear coach, Steve Chandler, for patiently reminding me to slow down—again and again! Thanks for reading and responding to countless e-mails. Also, thanks for guiding my reading and for reconnecting me with the timeless aspect of who I am. I take odd pride in the knowledge that we were both writing books about time at the same time!

Thanks to my friends for supporting my dreams daily, including Ala, Kay, Melanie, Joanne, Mimi, Robin, and Amy. Love and thanks to my mother and sisters, strong women all.

Thanks to those at Argosy University of Dallas, The Dallas REBT CBT Meetup, and The Dallas Club Fearless Meetup. You hold me to a high standard and this pushes me to do my best in your presence.

Finally, thank you to my therapy patients and coaching clients for your courage and for using the suggestions in this book. It is a big step to reach out for help.

To my readers: I hope this book and the examples in it are something you can use as a part of your own work, to keep you focused on what is IN your control.

Foreword

A ruthless, but gentle guidebook

Pam Garcy has achieved a neat trick with this useful book. She has revealed some of the most refreshingly tough-minded principles I've seen for time-creation, and done so in such a folksy, gentle way that we are not intimidated.

She sees the real problem early: it's not time itself, but our stories about time. Not true limitations, but our limited beliefs. And by so clearly identifying the source of chaos as being in the mind of the beholder, she then moves to gentle, useful prescriptions for uncluttering life.

Dr. Pam Garcy is a respected psychologist whose book, The Power of Inner Guidance has been a favorite of mine for long while. She understands the power of inner wisdom as a true guide to a fulfilled life. It's the road less traveled by most. Most people, in my own experience as a coach and corporate trainer, live inside the anxiety of outer approval-seeking. Inner wisdom is unknown territory. But this book is a great start for appreciating its practical value.

This book guides us back inside to find the priorities we want to have. From those priorities, the creation of the day unfolds.

Dr. Garcy uses a wonderful story, almost a parable, of rocks, pebbles and sand, to make the process of time management easy to for the mind to picture and grasp.

I'm usually not a fan of books that contain exercises for me to do. But the exercise that arrives in the middle of this book about making time is intriguing: What if you only had a week to live? What would you do? Who would you want to be with?

Dr. Garcy's hidden point is unforgettable: we do, as far as we know, only have a week to live. Why not live that way? Why not live with that kind of deep enjoyment and completion? No one is even guaranteed tomorrow, yet we live as if there is no end to things. We don't see that limitations are what give time its sense of being precious.

Dr. Garcy shares a case history with a patient named Tina that dramatizes what it is to truly prioritize, and what happens when we do. It's this combination of peeks into the world of psychotherapy and down-to-earth folk wisdom from a friend (such as the four D's: Do, Delay, Delegate and Dump) that make this book so user-friendly and compelling.

There's some deep meaning in the title of this wonderful book, *How to Make Time When You Don't Have Any*. Because most people believe time is linear and finite and always in stressfully short supply. And that there's nothing we can do about it. The tools here actually give the reader a way to transcend the illusion of not having any time. This book provides mental tricks and systems to "make" or create fresh, new amounts of time, non-linear in nature, and precious enough to contain everything you really, truly want to do. I will be recommending this book to my time-stressed friends and I know you will too.

Steve Chandler
Phoenix, Arizona
September, 2010

Chapter 1 – The Stories You Tell About Time

When I was in graduate school, I was quite fond of saying the phrase "I don't have enough time."

Hurried to the max, trying to complete all of my assignments and not knowing how to juggle it all, I used to take morbid delight in complaining that I *never* had *any* time.

Underlying this, I felt helpless. I knew that getting through the training program was crucial to reaching my goals. Yet, I didn't know how to negotiate all of the readings, reports, and tests. How could I create balance? I hoped that there was a solution to the problem that I was seeing. I began to look for a different way.

Comparing myself to one of my classmates, I noticed some differences between her quality of life and my own. She'd take breaks on the weekends. She'd go on long walks around White Rock Lake with her dogs. She'd get her laundry and grocery shopping done with regularity. Sometimes, she painted beautiful pictures. Other times, she went on bike rides, took naps, and went to parties.

It seemed like she had time to do her homework and then some. What was it about her? As intelligent as she was, she didn't seem to be any more capable of managing the enormous amount of schoolwork than I was. We seemed to be equally matched—in fact, she sometimes asked me for help. So, I couldn't understand how she managed to live such a balanced life in the midst of so much homework. How come I studied all weekend, while she seemed to have plenty of time to organize, play and rest?

Back then, I didn't know (but I was learning) that it was the *story* that I was telling myself about time that was preventing me from enjoying my time. Due to ideas that I believed and mentally reviewed, I was completely "stressed out," making graduate school a lot harder than it needed to be.

What stories do you tell yourself about your time? Read the list below and see if you say any of these things to yourself or others:

1. I would do that, but I don't have any time.
2. I'm too busy to do that.
3. I can't do that because I'm swamped.
4. I've always wanted to _____, but I don't have any time for that.

5. That's for kids—once you're an adult, there's no time for that.
6. There's so little time!
7. I feel so rushed all the time.
8. I can't get it done now.
9. There's no way I can fit ____ in, even though I want to.
10. How can I possibly get it all done?

Perhaps you even have some other phrases that you say to yourself about your time, your ability to get things done, and your ability to make choices about what activities you'll pursue.

In my private psychology and coaching practice, I hear this often. People come in, sometimes in tears. They explain that they have too much to do and that they cannot take care of themselves due to a lack of time. Unfortunately, they feel helpless to make changes that they say they'd like to make.

Other people come in describing that they have a hard time saying "no". These folks add an additional set of statements onto their story about time.

Do you elaborate upon your story with any of the following ideas?

1. Service to others is more important than taking care of myself.
2. If someone asks me, I cannot say "no" to them or let them down.
3. If I say "no," there won't be anyone else who can do this.
4. I feel important and happy when I volunteer, serve, or help others—so I must do it a lot if I want to feel good about myself.
5. I need others to appreciate me, which they'll do when they notice how much I'm doing.
6. If I don't put in all the hours that I'm asked, others will disapprove of me, talk badly about me, or stop asking me to be a part of things.
7. Others (children, parents, friends, etc.) are reliant upon me and would not be able to manage with any less of my time.

While it is wonderful and healthy to do things for others, it is important to have balance. If you volunteer, serve, and help others, you can acknowledge that this is of great value. It is also important, though, to recognize when the word "no" can become a service-oriented word too. "No" is the magic word which sets the boundary between "just enough" and "too much" for you. "No" is a word that can bring you balance, help you to self-pace, and prevent you from burning-out on contribution.

In writing this book, I spoke with several women who either are volunteering or were volunteers. During this process, I heard stories from many ex-volunteers who went "full force" and never said "no" to anything. Over time, this led to burn-out, and these individuals left volunteering altogether. I also know fabulous volunteers who have learned to say "no" as needed; they enjoy the pleasures of service in a balanced fashion, leaving them invigorated by the process for years.

Awareness Building Activities
In order to increase your own awareness and begin to reclaim your time, you'll notice that I have inserted awareness building activities in many of the chapters which follow. I have allowed space for you to jot your own ideas down, so you can return to them later, as your thinking evolves.

Let's start by evaluating the story that you're currently telling yourself about your time.

Below, write down some of the key phrases that you tend to say or believe about your time.

Chapter 2—Examining Your Roles and Tasks

Now that we've examined some of the phrases that you use to describe your time, we'll discuss your roles and tasks.

Examining your specific roles and tasks may also lead you to realize how you direct your focus. You will see that you are faced with many choices throughout your day.

When I am working with individuals with time challenges, one of the first things I usually hear from them is that they assume multiple roles; the roles are in conflict, there are multiple tasks within each role, and the tasks are often in conflict.

For example, a woman may wear many hats. She may be a daughter, a wife, a mother, a granddaughter, a niece, and a cousin. At work, she may wear the hat of supervisor, employee, and last-minute-pitch-hitter. Outside of work, she may be a student and a teacher, a volunteer and a party planner, a best friend and a coach, a housekeeper and cook. She may have hobbies which introduce the roles of singer in a choir, book club member, movie patron, theatre aficionado, concert enthusiast, and political activist. She may be author and reader.

Doing favors for others may lead her to adopt other roles from carpooler to hand-holder, and the list goes on! We could make a similar list for men as well, but I think we all get the point: there are so many roles that an individual may assume-- intentionally, through obligation, or by surprise.

To make matters worse, he or she may also be responsible for completing any number of time-consuming tasks within each role. These tasks and roles can conflict with each other and an individual must then decide which one will take priority. So, it is no wonder that at one point or another, many of us use the phrases, "I don't have any time," "I'm swamped," or, "I'm too overwhelmed."

The pie chart clarification technique

One technique from Cognitive Behavioral Therapy (a type of therapy which I use with my patients) is a pie chart construction technique. The pie charts you'll draw will help you to look at how you're currently distributing your roles, tasks, and other aspects of your typical day.

Basically, to do this, you will construct two pie charts. Pretend that the pie represents your typical day, which contains a finite quantity of time. First, you'll construct a chart that conveys how your day is accurately divided, labeling each piece of the pie. For example, if you spend half of your day on the phone and on your computer, phone and computer time would take 50% of the pie.

Next, you'll construct your "ideal" pie chart. This will help you to become crystal clear about what you'd like to create for yourself.

To make this clear, I will use my own pie charts as an example.

Before I drew my first pie chart, I knew that I wanted to play with my children more, I wanted to exercise more, and I wanted to have more fun with my friends. So, in order to do this, I had to take a fresh look at how I was dividing up my day.

This was how my pie chart looked initially—as I looked at it, I realized quickly that I was allocating far too much of my day to activities that were unproductive, and not enough time to those that were important.

My initial pie chart looked like this:

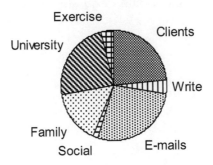

So, I created a pie chart which would expose what tasks I wanted to expand, and which ones I wanted to shrink. I learned that if I would decrease the amount of grading I was doing and reply with shorter response to emails, I could play with my children more, have more fun with my friends, and sit down to write at more normal hours. The pie chart technique helped me to figure out what I was working to create.

My ideal pie chart looked like this:

Ideal Allocation of Tasks

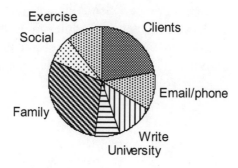

Now it's your turn. Construct a pie chart which shows your current activities in the circle below.

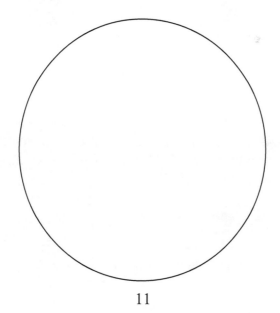

Next, construct the second pie chart. In this pie chart, construct your *ideal* allocation of your activities. Ask yourself what you'd like to do more. Look to see what you can do less. You can also add activities that you wish were in your schedule. You may also decide to reduce or eliminate other activities. Draw this in the circle below.

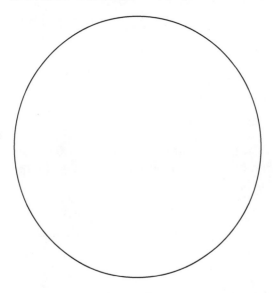

Use the ideal pie chart as a reference to what you'd like to create. Begin taking action to create your ideal.

Chapter 3—The Real Story

You may already be anticipating the idea I'm about to share. At the risk of being chastised, I'm going to introduce a somewhat iconoclastic question to ponder. Here it is: What if the idea that *you do not have any time to do what you really want to do* was only an idea, but not reality? What if the truth were that the concept of time was being misunderstood and misused, largely as a function of our language? What if we were to be brutally honest with ourselves about time? What might we begin to see?

In writing this book, this is what I did. I ran the idea of "not having any time" through what I call the "sieve of sanity," which I describe in my earlier books. The sieve of sanity is basically a set of questions which helps you to look at information with a scientific mindset.

Here is the question and answer process that occurred:

Is it true that someone can not have any time? It would be true if someone were about to die. In other instances, a person would still have time.

Is it true that some people have more time in a day than others? No. We each have 24 hours.

How would I feel if I told myself that I didn't have any time to do what I wanted to do? I would feel anxious, helpless, and even depressed.

How might I act if I believed I didn't have any time? I'd probably be rushing, multitasking, and working myself too hard. Inadvertently, all of these behaviors could decrease my productivity and even my efficiency. I might make careless errors or miss something important.

So, is it helpful to tell oneself that one doesn't have any time? In most cases, it probably is not.

Choice Management Instead of Time Management
Are there any other ways to look at this? Yes. I can look at this in terms of **choice management**, rather than **time management**. Time is finite. The variable component is choice. Choice implies freedom and power.

How might I *feel* if I told myself that I was going to work on managing my choices instead of my time? I'd feel hopeful, optimistic, excited, and rejuvenated! Choices are things that I can change—even when time is finite.

How might I *act* if I told myself that I was going to manage my choices instead of focusing on the constant—time? I would probably become more deliberate. I would take more action. I would work to reduce actions that weren't helpful. I'd realize that each day had room for several choices. I'd recognize that whether or not I chose to take an action, I was exercising my freedom. Even a non-choice would be a choice for me. It would mean that I was picking the default. The entire mentality of choice would lead me to speak and respond differently—as someone who is at the wheel, rather than in the back seat.

What if you were to gradually relinquish the idea that you didn't have time and start to focus upon managing your choices instead? What might begin to happen for you?

In order to redirect your thinking in this way, it might be helpful to start by reminding yourself that we all have a fixed quantity of 24-hours in a day. You don't actually get more hours in a day than I do. I also don't get more hours in a day than you do.

If you then temporarily suspend your current focus upon the scarcity of your time and instead only look at time as a reference point for your CHOICES and PRIORITIES, you'll begin to realize that the phrase "I don't have any time," is actually disempowering you. Sometimes, it is more accurate and helpful to say that you haven't fully exercised your power to choose.

So, ask yourself if any of the following is a more accurate reframing of what is happening:

(1) you believe that you have too many tasks to complete,
(2) you have agreed to simultaneously perform too many roles,
(3) you are too willing to take on any additional tasks, especially those that are not a true priority to you,
(4) tasks may be in competition with one another for your prioritization
(5) you don't have the skill set to complete a specific task by a specific deadline
(6) you think that you cannot say "no" to a request

If you are already beginning to subtly reframe your language, then the traditional term, "time management," might be replaced with "time-choice management," "choice management," or "power scheduling." All of these terms would imply that you are deliberately attending to that which is *in* your control.

Remember that because we are programmed through rules, and rules are based in language, some of our programming is semantic and even unconscious. Language has probably programmed your view of time. If so, you tend to unconsciously view time as a scarce commodity. When time is seen as a scarce commodity, you "spend" it, you "run out" of it, and you even get into situations when you think you don't "have any." When things aren't going as well as you'd like, you have "dead time" or you "kill time," in the effort to forget that you're "wasting time." This focus upon time-as-a-scarce-commodity is not wholly bad, but the programming can lead you to forget what *is* in your control—not the ticking of the clock, but the choices you make between the ticks.

I therefore invite you to take a mental walk with me as you read this book. We will walk away from the idea of "time-as-a-scarce-commodity," "time scarcity," and thereby "time management." Instead, we'll stay away from language which elicits our fear—and replace it with language and ideas which elicit our awareness, motivating us to take action. This is the language of choice.

> **The embedded language
> of time-as-a-scarce-commodity**
>
> I spent my time…
> I wasted time…
> I killed time…
> I ran out of time…
> I don't have any time to ____.
> "Time management" or "time scarcity"
>
> **Potential problems:**
> Anxiety, resentment, panic, depression, guilt, lack of
> joy, lack of balance, hot/cold action (rushing or
> procrastination), avoidance behaviors

> **The conscious language
> of choice**
>
> I choose to ____
> I decide to____
> I want/desire/prefer to____
> I plan to ____
> I'll prioritize ____
> I'll pick ____
> I'll schedule ____
> I will **do** ____
> "Choice Management," "Time Choices,"
> and "Power Scheduling"
>
> **Potential benefits:** calm action, slowing down and
> enjoying your experience, mindfulness, flow, honesty
> with self and others, greater balance in life, approach
> behaviors, increased productivity

In this process, you may not be able to fully escape the language of time-as-a-scarce-commodity or time-scarcity. After all, it is so embedded and essentially automatic that it is challenging to even take a tiny step away from it.

Here's the good news: You don't have to totally get away from the use of this language, or permanently restrict your speech to the language of choice. *Temporary breaks* from this perspective are all that is needed! These mental breaks can be extremely valuable to your approach to time because they allow you to challenge your assumption of scarcity.

Using the language of choice, even if only for a few moments, can raise your awareness and allow you to see the possibilities which are *in* your control. To see what is currently invisible to you, you must put on a different set of lenses.

The skills you'll need
Developing a good set of time-choice skills will train you to focus upon that which you can control, rather than staying stuck in that which you cannot.

Although many skills can contribute to good time-choices and to a healthier mindset about time, the skills that are most crucial, in my opinion, would include identifying and taking ownership of choices that are in your control, clarifying your values, planning ahead, learning to pace yourself and take breaks, developing a system for follow-through, and becoming a master of your personal organizational style.

Let's talk about each of these now.

Ownership of choices means that it is helpful to start to take an honest look at the stories you tell yourself about your time (which you just did). Learning to challenge this story and to call parts of it "false," even as a matter of mental exercise, will lead you to recognize the freedom that you're allowing to slip away unnoticed.

Values clarification implies that you will take an inventory of what is important. There are questions that you are answering nonverbally already—you answer through your actions. How you live your life and what you strive to create are reflections of your values. In an upcoming chapter, we will go into more depth about values-based choices and management of these choices.

Your ability to *plan* relates largely to your own personal style. Some people are very organized and methodical, planning ahead, using planners or PDA's. Others go with the flow more, and yet have a general focus and continuity to their movement which helps them to become very efficient and effective. Still others are somewhere in the middle, making an occasional to-do list or using sticky notes. You may already know which style works best for you, or you may want to experiment with other styles.

Related to this is the ability to *self-pace*. Sometimes, people don't understand how long a task will take and in this regard they underestimate or overestimate the amount of time that it will take to complete the task. In the case of procrastination for example, people tend to underestimate the amount of time it will take for them to complete the task and they tend to overestimate their capability for timely task completion. In this regard, they also start tasks too late to allow adequate completion with regard to followthrough and organization. Others drive themselves too hard and never take breaks, paying the toll for the chronic use of this lack of pacing. Learning tricks for self-pacing and taking breaks can become critical to health and sanity, not to mention instrumental in relaxed and productive living.

The commitment to *following-through* on the tasks that you decide are most important, not getting distracted and staying on task, and staying organized within the process are key factors to timely task completion. Organization is important so that you can find what you need without too much distraction.

Finally, it is important to *communicate and delegate*. If you are working with others, are you in communication with these others so everybody knows exactly what is going on? Is there a plan with deadlines in place for various components of the task? Can you count on your team?

Also it is important for you to evaluate what is the best time-choice and recognize whether you could delegate certain tasks to others. There are people who have great difficulty delegating tasks to others due to distrust for how others might do the job. Such individuals have a high need for control of the external, which is a fear-based response.

You may wonder why it is fear-based. It is fear-based because if you trusted your own abilities and you knew that you could count on *you* no matter what events happen outside of you, then you could worry less about the potential failings of others, and you could give others an opportunity to try and help you. You would probably be careful selecting the person who would help you, give that person the tools to help you effectively, provide feedback as needed, and allow the person to help you. In the worst case you'd trust that you would pick up the pieces.

This attitude and skill set would give you the freedom, flexibility, and potential rewards of delegating certain tasks to others. Ultimately, the skills which help you to manage your time-choices well are not the sole focus of this book. What is more important than these skills is recognizing how important your ideas about time are to this entire process.

Your mindset can either help you to enjoy the process of working within your power or can keep you focused upon what is outside of your power.

The rest of this book is devoted to revisiting the idea that you don't have any time as you reclaim your day, shine light upon your choices, empower yourself, and develop new ways to live a productive and full life!

Chapter 4 – The Full Fridge

The other day I was cleaning out my refrigerator. Usually, this is part of my weekend chores. However, the weekend before, I'd goofed off. Yes, as much as I hate to admit this to you, it had been a couple of weeks. I know...gross.

Even so, I was actually quite amazed at how much had accumulated. There were containers full of leftovers for later eating, expired yogurts, cups of half-consumed chocolate milk, almost full juice boxes that kids had sipped, previously fresh herbs and veggies that I thought I'd use but didn't, and even near-empty containers of condiments. I felt a bit disappointed, seeing what we'd wasted.

What was great, however, was to be reminded of the things that hadn't spoiled and to realize that there were items that I hadn't opened and which we could still enjoy. The thing is, I wouldn't have been able to find the good stuff if I have not cleaned up the bad stuff.

Sometimes, these seemingly haphazard events of life contain lessons which apply to other areas. How could my packed refrigerator relate to the discussion of time?

It relates with the idea of TOO MUCH.

Sometimes we accumulate too much. TOO MUCH forces us to neglect what we've taken and to waste what is already there.

Sometimes, less is more. We can focus on what we really want, really use it, clear it out, and then get more.

Hoarding and saving creates distraction and eliminates clarity. Instead, we are overwhelmed, confused, and drained of energy when we look at how much is before us.

Do you put too much in your schedule, or overbook yourself thinking that an opportunity will be missed? In the meantime, do you neglect other opportunities that are already there, and end up disappointed with the wastefulness?

If so, clean out your planner, just like you'd clean out your fridge. Cancel activities that no longer serve you. Delegate some jobs to others. Resituate events so that you can develop a healthier balance in your life. Just as doing this with your fridge helps you to see things more clearly, doing this with your planner will help you to develop clarity and perspective.

Have You Lost Sight of What's Really Important?

Think back over the past year…

"Fridge" list:

Have you made a new friend?
Have you grown closer to an old friend?
Have you given a party?
Have you had a discussion about a great book?
Have you learned a new song?
Have you challenged yourself to stretch?
Have you done something you've always wanted to do?
Have you really stopped and listened to each person in your family?
Have you loved a pet?
Have you created something new?
Have you "gone for it"?
Have you asked for what you want?
Do you express appreciation to others?
Have you given charity?
Have you hugged those you love?

If not, what excuse are you using
to hold yourself back
from living all out?

Chapter 5 – Start With The Most Important

A popular metaphor, whose source is unknown, tells the story of rocks, pebbles, and sand.

Though there are several versions, one version of the story goes that there was once a professor who came into his class and said, "Here are some rocks, some pebbles, and some sand. Our job is to put them all into this big jar over here."

First the professor poured in some sand. Then he poured some pebbles, and then he tried to put the big rocks into the jar. Unfortunately, not all the big rocks could fit. The professor said, "Can anyone else give it a try?"

A few students approached the front of the room. They tried to add the large rocks to the jar, using various angles and pressure. None of them could get them all the large rocks to fit. "We can't—there isn't enough space."

Next, the professor said, "Let's try a new approach." He removed the rocks from the jar, next the pebbles, and last the sand, putting each of these into containers on the side. Now once again, he was left with a big empty jar.

The professor looked thoughtfully at the students, "Before we try this new approach, does anyone have any ideas about how we will get all of this into the jar?" The students looked perplexed at the cryptic question—hadn't they just proven that it was impossible? They snickered, wondering how the professor thought he could fit everything into the jar, big though it seemed. No one spoke…it was probably a trick. "Okay," the professor said simply, "Watch."

He then took the big rocks and put them into the jar first, next he poured in the pebbles, and finally he poured in the sand. Everything fit into the jar beautifully.

The professor said, "The jar is like your life. The big rocks represent the big and important things in your life. These are the things that are critical to your health and your happiness. The pebbles are less important but necessary. The sand is the rest. If you make room for the most important things, you will have room for everything else. Start with the most important."

The story illustrates how the simple act of consciousness and prioritization allows us to become intentional about what we put into the jars of our lives. When we are conscious about our scheduling, we put the important things "first" in line. Then, we allow the next important things to enter. The minutiae can fill into the crevices which remain, and somehow it all fits together naturally.

When we are unconscious about our days, and when we do nothing to systematically remove our unconsciousness, we will be left with a costly outcome. We'll wonder why there is not room for the important things in life. Space runs out, and we are left wondering and perplexed, declaring that we are helpless and that our tasks are impossible to complete.

What will you put it into your jar first, the rocks, the pebbles, or the sand? Have you been filling your jar with sand first? Have you been taking time to remember the big rocks, or are the pebbles and sand getting in your way?

Sit down for a moment and list what you consider to be the rocks of your life. The rocks are represented by what is most important to you--the things that you want to make sure to put into your life.

MY "ROCKS"

For me, this includes spending time with my husband and children every day, taking time to exercise and meditate, good nutrition, a healthy household, and taking good care of my patients and clients.

Next, answer this: What are your pebbles? The pebbles represent things that are important, but not as important as the rocks of your life.

MY "PEBBLES"

For me, the pebbles of life include staying connected to my extended family, spending time with my friends, keeping in contact with business contacts, working on longer term projects, connecting with others in the community, contributing through volunteering, and maintaining a generally clean and smoothly run household (most of the time).

Last, answer this: What is the sand in your life? The sand is symbolic of the things in your life which will somehow find a space, but which are best left unscheduled and are not prioritized.

MY "SAND"

For me, I discover the sand daily. At times, the sand is shown in the unpredictable things that "come up" for me during a day.

If you are the type to use a planner or PDA, this metaphor is especially effective. Although you may have to page forward in your calendar or PDA, you can decide to implement this procedure as soon as possible. You can sit down with your planner and make sure that you schedule in the rocks of your life first—the things that are most important. Then, write in the things that are of secondary importance. Finally, allow the least important things to fill in the spaces, either through planning or through the natural rhythm which happens when you respond to life from a position of ease. Check off the following list as you accomplish this task. (You may have to start this several weeks down the road.)

My checklist
I've scheduled my rocks first I've schedule my pebbles second I've scheduled in the predictable "sand" I can see where other "sand" might fit

You may say that you have various obligations that are preventing you from putting in these things that you consider to be most important.

Do you remember what the professor had to do when his jar was filled with sand first? He had to empty the jar and start over.

This may not be a luxury that you presently have. However, you might be able to shift the sand out of the way, even if only temporarily, so as to renegotiate your positioning of your rocks.

32

If these obligations cannot be shifted, do your best to see where they will fit—but change your schedule as soon as you can. As I mentioned earlier, even if you turn several pages into your calendar, or move forward in time several weeks on your PDA, your goal is to schedule your rocks first. YOU decide what is presently among your rocks.

Perhaps you have an obligation, such as a job, which you do not see as a rock. You feel helpless and victimized—how could your time have been "used up" by something that isn't a priority to you?

If you take issue with the idea that the obligation is a rock, then what you're really telling yourself is that you are not the person calling the shots in your life. Is this really true, or are you CHOOSING to move in a way that is incongruent with your values and priorities?

If you stop and look at yourself in the mirror, and you truly say, "I'm the one who chooses," then you'll begin to see if you are living in way that is incongruent with your values and priorities. If you are doing this, you are living *out* of integrity.

To live *in* integrity and to learn how to listen to yourself more fully I would refer you to my book, ***The Power of Inner Guidance***, which helps you to tune in and figure out exactly what you want to do with your life, both moment to moment and over the long-term. This book will help you to learn to listen to your inner guidance along the way. It will teach you a process for making decisions which are in unity with your heart and mind. To learn more about this book and hear free teleseminars that I conduct, you can visit my site at http://www.myinnerguide.com.

You can also sign up for my free online e-zine, *Insourcing*, which supports you taking control over your life despite what anyone else may be telling you. To sign up for this newsletter, please visit http://www.myinsourcing.com.

Chapter 6 – The Common Cold Versus The Flu

Have you ever walked around with a cold, simply neglecting yourself and neglecting that your body is telling you that you are a little bit worn out and a little bit rundown? You do this so that you can continue to get things done.

You don't want your cold to stop you from accomplishing the tasks that are on your list. Often, you can get away with continuing to push yourself when you have a cold. So, a common cold, even though it is a signal, can run its course relatively ignored. Unfortunately, the quiet lesson behind the common cold is easily ignored.

What about the flu? Sometimes if you have the flu, you don't really have the strength or motivation to continue to get things done. In fact, due to various endogenous pyrogens, you may find that you physically shut down due to the effects of fever. You're forced to lie down and heal. As a matter of fact, you might crave sleep and fluids more than anything else.

When you return to work after the flu, you might feel shaky. Moreover, a sudden conscientiousness emerges. You notice yourself getting to bed on time (no matter what). You become alert to the fact that staying as healthy as possible is a prerequisite for all of the other things you want to do. It is hard to escape the lesson of the flu, because the lesson is loud and clear: You'd better take care of yourself!

When you are almost forced to take a week or two off, you somehow resume where you left off. How can that be?

While work has built up, somehow things have managed to continue and life has managed to go on. While not minimizing your importance, the flu tells you, "Get real." It helps you to see that it is equally important to recognize that taking good care of yourself affords you the privilege of being able to contribute to humanity. In addition, taking care of yourself increases your potential for longevity.

As important as you are to others, the *things* that you think are so pressing and urgent may occasionally have to be delegated or put on hold. Sometimes, we start to buy into a story that no one else can do the job, no one else will do it with love, and that our work must be done with immediacy and only the way we would do it.

While it is sometimes true that no one else can do your work the way you would, we very often extend this reality well beyond what is really true, using it to disturb ourselves about taking helpful and self-supportive steps—steps which are essential for our physical and emotional wellbeing. When we buy into this story, we'll find that we drive ourselves crazy with guilt, shame, fear, and blame whenever we want to take some time to ourselves.

In this respect, how often do you put off scheduling a respite or vacation for yourself? Do you secretly tell yourself that you are too essential to take a break, that projects will collapse without you, or that a vacation isn't necessary for you (even though it is okay for other people)?

If this is you, then I have a question for you: Have you ever noticed that people who hold onto this mindset don't take vacations? And have you ever noticed that these same people may eventually find that their bodies are exhausted or immunocompromised? If they don't give themselves breaks and don't take care of themselves, what tends to happen? They tend to take another type of vacation--they get sick. I believe that in *certain* instances, getting sick is your body's way of taking over and forcing a vacation (of sorts).

If you've seen this too, then you have two choices: you either take an occasional vacation or the vacation takes you.

The related question becomes, "How can I take a vacation without feeling guilty?" The answer is to recognize (1) the power of vacations to help you to remain energized and available over the longer term and (2) the fact that if you had the flu, others would have to find a way to cope with your temporary absence.

What is better than getting stressed out, immunocompromised, or sick might be to prepare others to take over specific tasks in your job, and to then schedule vacations for yourself. You will find that not only will others learn to work around your vacations, but *you too* will find your way around them—and you may find that the value in the breaks makes all of the extra effort totally worth it!

Chapter 7 – A Week To Live

How are you doing on our little mental walk? I hope you're learning something new or getting reminded of something that is important to you.

Now, I'm going to ask you to do a reflective exercise, so grab a pencil or pen. Get into a quiet and peaceful place where you can hear yourself think. Now, settle in and allow yourself to relax. Take some slow and deep breaths. Just for a moment, let go of any worries, and focus upon this exercise. You can return to your worries when you're done, if you'd like!

So, here are the questions upon which I suggest you contemplate and write:
1. If you only had a week to live, AND if you had a magic wand which allowed you to wave away any obstacles, **what** would you do during the week?
2. Whose company would you make sure to enjoy?
3. What are the things that you would make sure to do?
4. What would you blow off?

Take the next few pages to journal about what you would do if you only had a week left to live.

Take a few moments and journal any answers that emerged:

What did you learn from this exercise?

What have you been procrastinating doing in your life? What would you like to take steps to start doing more?

```



```

If there is something stopping you from doing this, can you identify the obstacles?

```






```

Identify which of these obstacles you've just listed are within your control to remove or modify. Put a check next to these.

Next, construct a preliminary plan for removing or modifying these obstacles. Remember that it is okay to get help and use your resources. Write a preliminary plan below. How will you incorporate your big ideas into your daily life?

```






```

Other thoughts/ideas:

Chapter 8 – What Have You Made The Priority?

Here's another concept that I seem to keep rediscovering in my work with clients: if you're not doing something that you say you want to do, it is because you haven't made it the priority. In addition, you may not be doing something because you think it is in conflict with your values—but very often the thing you're putting off is what is most in support of your values.

I'll illustrate this point with a couple of case examples below. Please note that whenever I give case examples, identity details are **well disguised** so that you won't be able to recognize who I am referring to.

Case example #1: Financial Security
Saied was a 25-year-old coaching client. He approached me because he had credit card debt.

I asked Saied, "What is the problem that you are having?"

He said, "I have this…credit card debt and I have not paid it off. I want to pay it off," he said, looking down.

I asked, "Why haven't you paid it off?"

44

He said, "Well I just, I don't know how to do it."

I said, "Well, I'm not a financial adviser, but wouldn't you just start paying as much as you can afford to pay?"

He said, "Well actually I could pay it all off tomorrow."

"Oh?" I looked at him curiously.

Saied said, "I have lots of land and money in savings. Technically, I could pay it all off tomorrow. But, I don't feel good paying it off."

I asked, "Could you explain that to me a bit more?"

Saied said, "It makes me uncomfortable to carry debt."

Once again, I said, "I don't really understand the problem. If you have the money and if debt feels uncomfortable, then what's preventing you from getting yourself out of this discomfort?"

Saied said, "Well, I would like to keep all of my money in the bank. I'd like to keep all of the land I have rather than sell it. So I don't see how I could pay it off and keep everything else as it is.

"Saied," I said, "What have you made the priority?"

He said, "What do you mean?"

I said, "Well if your problem is credit card debt, and you truly wanted to solve this problem, and you became committed to solving this problem, it would be very easy for you; you'd pay off the credit card tomorrow. But, it doesn't sound like that's presently your priority."

Saied thought for a moment and said softly to himself, "What have I made the priority? What is more important than paying off this debt?" He paused. "I suppose it would be keeping the money in the bank and continuing to hold onto my land. Financial security, I guess."

"That is how I see it too," I said, "You have made all those things more important than paying off the credit card debt. These represent your priority: financial security. So, just to review this then, if paying off the credit card debt was really a priority to you then you would pay off the credit card debt, right?"

"Yes," Saied replied, already moving onto his next thought, "But isn't it wrong to carry around debt?"

"I think that since you want to make your financial security the priority, a more helpful question to ask might be whether or not it makes financial sense to do so. Acting in a manner that makes financial sense will give you more financial security. So, have you sat down with a calculator to find out what is the most financially wise decision for you?"

"Explain what you mean by that," Saied looked confused.

"Well, look at the whole picture—not just a piece of the puzzle. So, for example, is it more profitable to continue to have the credit card debt, because you are getting a higher return on the investment of the borrowed money than you pay out in interest? Or does it make more financial sense to let go of the debt?"

Saied agreed, "I realize what you mean now. My priority is financial security, but I am focused on only one piece of the puzzle. If I will look at the whole picture and take a few minutes with the calculator, the best decision will follow. And the decision will be in conjunction with whatever I make the priority. This feels much better to me."

Like Saied, you can apply this rule: When you have a conflict, start by asking yourself, "What have I made the priority? What is the real priority for me? How might what I *want* fit into my priorities?"

Saied wrote to me later, "I realized that whatever I have made the priority is what is being allowed to exist, so that there is really is not a problem. You were right—it was a question of prioritization."

"What have you made the priority?" is a simple but powerful question that I often ask my clients early in coaching. In addition, I ask this question to some of my therapy patients, as you'll see below.

Case Example #2: Taking Care of Others
In my work as a therapist, I often help people to gain motivation and to take action. Sometimes, the very action that they are retracting from is the action that they most need to take. For example, a person who abuses alcohol may feel hugely depressed and drink to escape depression. However, the alcohol itself adds to the depressed mood. So, elimination of the alcohol is often needed to clear the depression. Another example follows in the case below.

Once, I had a patient who we'll call Tina. Tina was a young woman who came to me because she said that she was having problems quitting smoking. Tina said, "If I don't quit smoking soon I am going to develop lung cancer like my mother did."

I said, "Talk more about your desire to *keep* smoking."

She thought for a moment and said, "I don't really want to keep smoking. I just do."

Guess what I asked her? You're right. I said, "Well, what have you made the priority?"

"What do you mean?" she answered. "I don't have time to quit smoking. I have other things on my schedule. I have work and things to do for my family. I have exercise that I would like to do, although lately I am not very good at it because I am out of breath. But I have other things to do. You see, I have relatives who are coming in town to visit. I have to entertain them. When am I supposed to quit smoking?"

I was quiet for a minute and took a deep breath, to slow myself down so that I wouldn't get caught up in Tina's whirlwind. "Tina, what you just answered has told me your priorities. Your priorities are your family, your job, your guests, and completing tasks related to taking care of them."

I paused and watched her nodding. I continued, "When your priority becomes quitting smoking, you will quit smoking."

She said, "How can I make that priority?"

I said, "Start by remembering the priority you have—taking care of others. If you realize that you cannot take care of others if you are very ill, then it is very simple to put quitting smoking first on your list."

"That's true," she smiled, "So…I, just put it first, above all of the people I have to take care of?"

"How well will you take care of them if you are ill?" I asked.

"Not well. But, I am struggling with the idea of how to put it first."

"When something is *the* priority, you put it first, as soon as you recognize that it is the priority. At first, you'd be working with the fact that you've already made other commitments with your time. However, as soon as you possibly could, you'd place that on your agenda. This would be something you'd start doing, and then you could start taking action steps in that direction."

"Right, right," she nodded with resolution. "It seems so clear all of a sudden. I'm going to take the next step and put it first!"

Four weeks later, she was well involved in the process of quitting smoking. Her doctor had given her a medication that was helping her to diminish the cravings. She was using some of the techniques I was suggesting, including limiting when she smoked and gradually reducing the frequency and amount of cigarettes. In addition, she'd found a support group for those who were in the process of quitting smoking.

She said, "Really the key thing was that I never realized that taking care of myself was consistent with my other priority, taking care of others. Also, I didn't see that I was *not* making it a priority and that is why it was not getting done!"

Clarity is Power. Take a moment to journal your answers to the questions which follow. As you gain clarity, you will find yourself freer to take more of the actions that you truly want to take.

What do you really want to do that you're not doing?

What have you made the priority?

If you could place a category label on the things you've made a priority, what would you categorize this as?

How does what you want to do support the category of priorities which you've just defined in the last question?

Chapter 9 – 4 D's and a C

<u>The Four D's</u>
Once I was complaining to my mastermind sister about not having enough time to make my first book into a best-seller.

"Pam," she said, "Haven't you ever heard of the four D's? It seems like they would help you right now."

"What are those?" I asked.

"Do, delay, delegate, and dump," she said.

"Tell me more!" I hadn't heard of this system.

She said, "Well, you make your list of what you need to do. Then, you sort through it. What things can you *do* today? What things can you schedule for another day or *delay*? Who can you *delegate* to take care of some of these tasks? Are there some tasks that you can *dump* and not do at all?"

This began to make sense to me. For example, I started to think about how capable my kids were and how they could help me with doing some chores around the around. I started to think about certain things that I was doing right away that really didn't need to be done right away and I started to think about things that I didn't need to be doing at all.

Yes, it is also true that some of the things that used to seem so crucially important started to fade in importance—they could be dumped. For example, while I still make my bed (well usually) I don't always throw the cushions on or make it look as fancy as I could. Sometimes, I just close it and get on with my day!

The C

What about the C? In this case, "C" stands for communicate. The term communication is something that most people find important but it's so overused that it's easily devalued in its importance.

When it comes to making right use of your time-choices, communication is one of the important skills you can have.

When I was intern, I worked at a place called the Dallas County Youth Village. I was the only psychology person there and I was responsible for the psychological well being of the 80 residents within. Dallas County Youth Village was made up of boys who were ages 9 to 15. Most of them had committed several crimes and were being incarcerated for longer periods of times. The place was based upon a level system.

Children had to work their way up through the level system prior to earning their release and to being re-integrated into society. It was important for me to do a good job. I felt very passionate about it, and the kids' faces and problems were on my mind from the minute I'd wake up to the time I'd go to sleep. Adding to my passion for doing a good job was the work of our director at that time, Mr. Mercer.

Mr. Mercer was an ambitious man. He could see the children as whole people. While others were walking around in a state of hopelessness, Mr. Mercer was optimistic. He knew that we could make a contribution that could permanently change the outcome of the lives of many of these boys.

So Mr. Mercer scheduled meetings, and in the meetings we talked passionately about what we would create for these kids. He'd entrance us with discussions about how we would treat them as whole people, how we would make sure that every part of their body was functioning to optimal health, how we would also treat their families while treating them individually, and how we'd help them interact with each other as a miniature community.

Many of these conversations were focused upon our work as a team. But, often I found that Mr. Mercer turned to me and asked me to contribute to various components of his overall plan. Because I saw the work as my own, and because I saw the need for psychological help, I was educating Mr. Mercer about all sorts of things that the Psychology Department (me) could offer.

Before I knew it, I was overwhelmed. Here's what I had on my plate: the request to do weekly individual therapy for each of these 80 boys, and to do group therapy for each of the cabins that they lived in, and to be available to provide family therapy, and to do evaluations before and after the boys would complete the program. How would I get it all done?

I sat down with my calendar and I created a master schedule as best as I could. I tried to accommodate all of the things that Mr. Mercer wanted done and quickly I realized that with 80 boys and just me it wasn't going to happen.

To me, there were two choices at that moment. I could make it my priority to complain and seek mercy or sympathy from others. Or I could communicate with Mr. Mercer about what was going on and what we would need an order to make his vision a reality. I chose to do the second.

I scheduled an appointment, and even though I was only an intern, I sat down across from this powerful man and showed him my schedule. I said, "Mr. Mercer, I really want to do everything that you said. I think that everything you said is extremely important for the boys."

He nodded. I said, "Here is my challenge and I would like you to help me with it."

He said kindly, "I am here to help."

Relieved, I continued, "This is what I see could potentially happen during that time. If it is possible for me to see these many boys each day, if I run a group every day each cabin will receive group therapy. In addition, I will be able to treat these many boys individually every day. In addition, I will have time to do one evaluation a week. After that, I also will need some time to dictate notes, to score the evaluations and write reports. So, Mr. Mercer, I am not quite sure where these other tasks that you like to have done will fit in my schedule. Can you please help me figure this out?"

Mr. Mercer looked at my master schedule and he said, "You know, you are absolutely right. This is far too much work for one person. We need to bring in another person to help you. I am going to bring in a lady who is a student in training, and you will supervise that student during one of your hours. The rest of these tasks will be delegated to her. That way between the two of you, you can work as a team and get more done."

I was so grateful. I said, "That sounds like a great idea, Mr. Mercer! I am going to make a schedule for her so that when she starts here, she can hit the ground running."

Mr. Mercer thought that was great. So I quickly sat down and constructed a schedule. Bad news was that as I did this, I realized that it didn't matter if both of us were working full force; we still wouldn't complete all the tasks that Mr. Mercer had laid out ahead of us.

So, I scheduled another meeting with Mr. Mercer and showed him the dilemma. Yes indeed, we actually needed three additional people not just one. So Mr. Mercer worked with the County Juvenile Department and arranged for a total of three students to train at our facility every week with me. They were my team and together we were helping these children to get to a place of better mental health.

The key point is that this would not have happened if I was not willing to communicate, and if I didn't have skills to communicate effectively.

If you're not up to communicating effectively, simply because you have some hesitation about being assertive or you don't have the skill set, then it is time to address these issues. This one particular issue is so important that it could completely hold you back from doing all of the things that you really want to accomplish. So if you want to have real power and effectiveness it is time to master this skill.

I often find that some of the most powerful work I do with my clients includes improving attitudes and skill sets surrounding communication. I have seen marriages changed, careers improved, friendships healed, support garnered, and stress markedly reduced through the simple use of effective communication strategies. In fact, communication is so important to your energy, health, and effectiveness that I want to invite you to write to me about your own struggles in this area. If you would like to obtain my special report called "Communication Tips for Effectively Working through a Conflict" ($27 value), you can write to me at drgarcy@aol.com and tell me about a struggle you're having with communication--I'll send these tips free of charge!

Chapter 10 – Speeding It Up

Speeding it up is a great strategy for getting certain tasks done in short bursts of time. For example when my family and I are cleaning the kitchen I generally set a timer for 20 minutes.

I'll say, "Let's see if we can get it all done before the timer goes off! Ethan, clear the table. Brittany, you rinse the dishes and load the washer. Max, you wipe up. Dad & I will put the food into the fridge. Let's see if we can do it!"

Together we work and work rapidly in order to get it done before the timer goes off. It becomes a game and involves team effort, which makes it fun instead of drudgery. Before we know it, our kitchen is clean and we are beating the timer!

Think of something at home or work that you can turn into a speed-game. Write down your ideas below.

Chapter 11 – Slowing It Down

When I was in kindergarten, I remember the teacher continually slowing us down. "Take your time," she'd say. "There's no hurry. It is more important to do a good job than to do it quickly."

Unfortunately, this lesson was quickly untaught as I progressed in school. Being fast and efficient was emphasized. We were given timed tests, and we were told that we probably wouldn't have enough time to finish. For the first time, I felt a sense of "pressure" and this pressure gave me the concept of time-scarcity, leading me to learn to hurry and feel rushed.

When a person is in a constant state of hurrying and rushing, they tend to focus so much upon the completion of an action that they forget to enjoy the process of completion. This can lead to a lack of pleasure and joy. The outcome is emphasized over the process, and the evaluation of the outcome is ongoing during the process. The person's consciousness is taken out of the action and misplaced on the clock.

So, sometimes, a reunion with your younger self reawakens your spirit. This self of early childhood did not know that time existed—

only that there was something magical to be done, and that the process of doing it was fascinating!

Slowing it down can actually become another technique that you can use to expand your time. How does this work?

When you slow things down, you become more mindful. You can breathe. You focus more easily. In this state, you are able to relax. You are able to invest yourself in the thing that you have in front of you. As a matter of fact, time is not even on your mind. You might become so engrossed in what you are doing that you forget to even look at a clock.

Time is not something that even readily occurs to you. When it *does* occur to you, the amount of time which has elapsed is often surprising. This is called the state of *flow* and in order to get there you start by slowing down.

How do you slow down? Start by telling yourself to do that which is in front of you slowly. Say it aloud if you like. (Believe it or not, this is a great thing to do when you are feeling rushed.)

After you decide to take things slowly, truly work to take it S-L-O-W. Pause between steps. Notice every detail around you. Get in touch with your senses.

What are you enjoying about this experience? Sometimes people don't want to admit how pleasurable it is to take their time...but, is there something fun about it? What do you notice? Journal your thoughts below for future reference.

Experiment with this the next time you think you deserve a little pleasure and want to be more efficient.

Chapter 12 – Attention Principles And Time

Principles of learning and attention reveal that what people focus upon tends to expand. If my son is making an obnoxious noise, and I tell him to stop, he tends to snicker and find another obnoxious noise. In paying attention to his bad behavior, I have grown it.

In the same way, when I thank my son for acting with such consideration and good manners, he is likely to do more of this in the future. What you pay attention to expands, and not only does it expand, you tend to prime yourself to notice more of the same.

So, you can prime yourself to notice specific states of mind and being, simply through the direction of your attention. If you notice someone yawning and then say the word, "Yawn," it becomes challenging *not* to yawn. You have increased your awareness for this action and its feelings, compelling your body to respond in kind.

By the same token, if you say the words, "I don't have any time," or if you allow yourself to believe that you don't have any time and then you complain about it, you are expanding your awareness to this state within yourself. You are making it more accessible to your awareness. In fact, this is what you pay attention to and this is what you think exists. It vigorously takes over your consciousness.

By virtue of this focus, you also tend to notice experiences which confirm your idea, and thereby *more of the same* becomes noticeable to you. You may even inadvertently create more of the same through your actions. For example, you may find you're hurrying and rushing and guess what happens? As you hurry and rush, you make careless mistakes. These mistakes lead you to have to undo and redo your steps. As a result, you inadvertently create more hurrying and rushing.

In relation to this, I recall once listening to a relaxation tape in which the author of the tape said the phrase, "There is so much time." Later in the tape, the phrase was repeated, "There is so some much, I have all the time I need, I have plenty of time."

I recognized that as I heard the tape, I was repeating the phrase to myself. In this repetition, I began to relax fully. I started to pay attention to the areas where I really did have time. I realized I had much more time than I was telling myself. I had so much time! Next time you're hurrying and rushing, see if you can shift yourself by beginning to notice how much time there actually is.

I have also found that my attention seems to bring me closer to things that are parallel with whatever I believe reality to be. For example, when I had my first baby, it seemed like everyone had babies all of a sudden. In psychology, this is called the "availability heuristic," and refers to how our perception can be affected by what is immediately available to us. So, if you'd like to have some control over this, you can use this awareness to direct your attention to what you want "available."

Using this concept, you might consider changing your mindset even more fully, by beginning a practice of being early. How? If you plan on being early with things, you will tend to experience finishing tasks in advance.

So, if you plan on being early to your drive to the airport, most likely you will arrive on time to the airport. Your intention to arrive early leads you to make plans to leave early, and your implementation of the plans often leads you to arrive early. Because your focus and attention is upon having plenty of time, you tend to find and create opportunities to get things done ahead of schedule, and to begin things as soon as the opportunity arises. This growing practice results in being early more and more often. You discover efficiencies and tend to use these to get things done in advance. Your awareness shifts from rushing to having plenty of time, and the overall shift leads you to feel calmer, more prepared, and generally more relaxed.

Chapter 13 – Task Expansion

The opposite of time expansion is task expansion. This is when the task expands to fit the time. Have you ever noticed that if you only have a certain amount of time to complete a task, this is how much time you will devote to the task?

However, when you have plenty of time to complete a task, the task tends to take all the time that is allotted for it. How can you use this awareness to enhance your efficiency?

Well if you keep in mind the task expands to fit the time and you use the concepts from chapter 10 of being early, then you will probably create a better outcome for yourself. Choose your desired outcome first by answering this question: When do you want the task completed? Then, create the responses around the outcome.

Here are some additional questions to answer: What will you have to do in order to complete your project ahead of schedule? Who will you turn to for help and support? What can you eliminate from the list of tasks that you have outlined? What aspects of the task completion are nonessential?

Chapter 14 – Blind Habits

When I was originally invited to speak on the topic of *how to make time when you don't have any*, I instantly recognized the scarcity model that was operating in the statement. As a result, I have to admit that I reacted with a bit of judgment, as the idea of not having *any* time was something that seemed unmistakably disempowered, helpless, victimized, and passive. The truth is that even though I liked the riddle behind the topic title, and I like just about any idea that leads to massively empowering others, the thought of not having *any* time was a paradigm that I did not truly subscribe to. I liked to think of myself as subscribing to the paradigm of choice, abundance, and personal power—not the paradigm of whining, complaining, and scarcity.

I realized that I was reacting to the topic a little too much. What was I bothering myself about? The more I considered the topic, the more I realized that the disempowerment beneath the title of this topic had to have an origin somewhere. My mind fantasized about the origin of this idea. Was it coming from a place of genuine pain within the audience with whom I'd be speaking? Or was it simply a cute idea that someone had, "Let's use a riddle for a title and stump the speaker!"

Did the committee have members that were stuck in this particular mindset? Or, did they know individuals who were coming to my talk who had this mindset; in the worst case, was the mindset prevalent among the people who they were reaching?

How could I really write an efficiency book, when I didn't see myself as an efficiency expert?

And if the mindset was prevalent, would the audience really be ready for an iconoclastic book—one which didn't focus exclusively on giving tips to manage their time—tips that couldn't possibly be entertained when one was still trapped in a scarcity model? One that was blunt about how holding onto such a model was simply a reflection of misguided thought? Did anyone even subscribe to this misguided thought? Or was I attacking a straw man?

In this contemplation process, I began to notice that there actually were people who were using this particular idea to run and govern their lives. There was nothing particularly wrong with those who used this idea, but there were certain obvious behaviors that people with time-choice issues seemed to habitually display.

For example, there was a handyman who used to work for us; he was a young fellow from Georgia. He was completely unaware of how he was conducting himself. Initially, he would spend so much time telling stories about his family that he could not get any work done. Then, when it came to completing the job he'd been hired to complete, he tended to need to leave. He'd say, "Oh--I don't have this equipment and I forgot to bring my other tools. I'll be back soon to finish this up."

His habit was so pernicious that I believed he probably continued to tell stories when he was supposed to be picking up the tools and engaging in less conversation. This would cause him to run so late that he was forced to return the next day. During the next scheduled work time, he would spend even more time complaining about how he didn't have any time, and time had "gotten away" from him. He'd blame others for his incomplete work, explaining how the people at the store had slowed him down.

Whining, complaining, and blaming are common bad habits of those who are injudicious with their schedules. If you believe that you don't have enough time, why would you then waste anymore of it with whining, complaining, and blaming?

Yet another blind habit is actually one which people believe will lead to greater efficiency: multitasking. But, the verdict is still out on multitasking. Recent research on the topic is suggesting that it leads to increased distractibility and diminished efficiency. So, think twice before you do two things at once!

The last blind habit I'd like to mention is simply the repetition of things that don't work. If you know that something doesn't work, then you can use this information to stop doing it. This will help you to shave off lots of mistaken actions, resulting in greater productivity. It is important for you to become aware of blind habits in your own life, be brutally honest, step back and find out what they are.

One of the fastest ways to find this out is to ask someone you trust. Others can see your blind spots with easy clarity!

Here are the Big Three efficiency-building questions that you can ask a supervisor, coach, or colleague to help you to eliminate blind habits:
1. What do you see that I'm *not* doing, that if I would do it would lead me to create much faster results?
2. Where do you see me being inefficient or unproductive?

3. What do you think I'm missing that
    could make my work go more
    smoothly and efficiently?

Record the answers to these questions
below.   Include a plan for counteracting
each of these blind habits.

Answer 1 and My Plan:

Answer 2 and My Plan:

Answer 3and My Plan:

Chapter 15 – Breaks And Efficiency

One of the number one reasons for succumbing to blind habits is that people don't take enough breaks. Just like vacations, if breaks are not taken with intention, you may find that you tend to take them in an unconscious and accidental fashion, leading to a less effective outcome.

Research confirms that breaks are important to overall efficiency. If you want to be efficient, it is important to schedule breaks into your day. At the other side of the issue, there are studies which suggest that overtime, even when it is only occasional, can lead to diminished productivity. So, having boundaries can actually help your efficiency and productivity!

Jenny was a client who was interested in learning to take breaks. She found herself becoming distracted by unimportant jobs, and she tended to substitute this blind habit for taking a real break. We discussed how this blind habit was *masking* her need for a mental re-set, and that it thereby compromised her productivity rather than enhancing it. At that point, she began to show some interest in taking breaks.

"How long of a break do I need to take?" Jenny asked.

"Well, there are different types of breaks," I explained. "The five-minute mini-break can be a just the right thing when you are in the midst of a very large workload; just take a moment and take a deep breath, go to the bathroom, get a drink. Basically, you want to remember that you are a human being, stretch your muscles, hydrate, and get back to work."

"What about lunch breaks? I'm not really sure what to do with mine and I end up working instead," she offered.

"A little break at lunch may actually be helpful for you, when you can take it," I suggested. "Can you take a break to eat and also take a little bit of a walk to re-energize and refresh? Then when you go back to work, you'll feel more engaged." I said.

"Okay," she agreed, "Should I do that every day? Should I make it a specific amount of time?"

"As far as I can tell from the research I've read, there is no single answer that applies to everyone—while it is agreed that breaks are good, it is important to determine how long of a break is right for you," I said.

"Let me explain a little more…if you were driving your car and your car's fuel indicator told you that it was almost out of gas, would you stop and fill up the gas tank before driving on—and if so, why?" I asked.

"Yes, because I'd feel really uneasy driving on empty because I wouldn't want to run out of gas," she said.

"And once your car is filled, then you'd pretty much feel *ready* to do a little bit more driving," I said. "Well, it is the same with breaks. Pay attention to when you're feeling like you're running out of energy. Then fill up so you'll feel ready to get back to what you were doing."

Like Jenny, you want to individualize your breaks. Regarding the length of breaks, you don't want to take so long of a break that you lose momentum and are not able to resume your task effectively and efficiently; however, it is a good idea to take breaks, to re-energize and refresh. Experiment with different amounts of time and see what works best for you.

Once in a while, it is important to take longer breaks. For example, Saturday nights are date nights for my husband and me. We work hard during the week and spend a lot of time with our children on the weekends, so it is important for us to take our time alone, away from our work and our children. This time allows us to have an uninterrupted conversation and relax together.

I know we already discussed the topic of vacations. However, in terms of the frequency with which you take a vacation as a break, I think it is important to do so every quarter. As a family, we generally take at least four trips a year. While the longer ones are more memorable, even a weekend getaway can help us to return with a refreshed outlook and perspective.

Chapter 16 – Accepting It

Dr. Albert Ellis was my personal hero when it comes to the field of clinical psychology. Dr. Ellis founded Rational Emotive Behavior Therapy, also known as REBT.

In REBT, we try to help clients to recognize that what they're telling themselves creates their realities. This is similar to what we were talking about in this book. In REBT, we not only look at the outer reality that the person is creating through their inner belief, but we also look at what emotions, behaviors, and physiological changes occur as a result of beliefs.

Ideas which you believe are seen as causal to emotions, behaviors, and physiology. Ideas that you don't believe lack power over you.

In addition, beliefs can be the effect of emotions, behavior, and physiology. All of these interact with each other. The belief is often the target point of intervention.

In REBT, we can intervene on the problem, the belief, the feeling, the behavior, or the physiology. Ellis found that intervention on the belief level can lead to philosophical shifts to core beliefs, and these shifts can permanently alter a person's way of being in the world. So it is not just the thoughts that frequently occur to us, but it is also those which we believe that tend to dictate our experiences and reactions.

Ellis talked about how *acceptance* is very key to driving beliefs that are healthy, whereas *non-acceptance* tends to drive beliefs that are unhealthy.

Non-acceptance is equated to an underlying philosophy in which one makes demands upon oneself, others, and life circumstances. So if you are in a state of non-acceptance and apply this to yourself, you might say, "I must be a fully functioning human being in all circumstances at all times, I must be effective and get everything done on time and not only that I must do it well. I must do it perfectly."

You would also have demands on others. "You must give me credit for all the hard work I am doing, you must affirm it, you must complement it, you must recognize it, and you must be here to help me make my life easier and do everything I need to do so that I can shine."

Moreover, you may have demands upon life circumstances, you might say, "My life must go the way I desire. Things must happen quickly and easily, the way that I want them to happen. Life must treat me fairly and this should be free from hassles."

Do any of these demands sound familiar?

When you are in a state of nonacceptance, these demands will lead you to *awfulize* (saying things are as bad as they possibly could be). It will also lead you to exhibit *low frustration tolerance* (you tell yourself you cannot be happy until your goal is met, leading to impatience). Lastly, it will lead you to *depreciate* yourself and others if you perceive either as standing in the way of task completion (in this context, depreciation means using labels to put someone down).

If you are operating from a place of acceptance, you will not have these demands or their derivatives. In fact, you will look at things relatively, you will say "I can only do the best I can and I accept myself for being a fallible human being."

To others, you'd say, "It is great if you help me and I really appreciate it when you do."

Regarding life, you'd realize that sometimes life circumstances prevent things from occurring as we prefer, and there are times when things had better be rescheduled.

Flexibility flourishes and rigidity washes away.

Instead of awfulizing, you'd start to see the whole picture, which is an anti-awfulizing perspective. So, you might say, "Things could be worse than they are now. It is very bad but certainly not the worst it could be."

Instead of low frustration tolerance, you'd exhibit high frustration tolerance, patience, and a commitment to your longer-term happiness (rather than short term gratification).

Instead of depreciation, you'd look at behavior. You wouldn't put yourself down, though you might recognize some behaviors which might benefit from improvement or correction. You wouldn't put others down, though you might see that some of their behaviors are inefficient or unfortunate.

Related to time, there are other aspects of acceptance that you will also recognize. With acceptance, you will also learn to accept time for what it is—a construct. You'd realize that you only have what time you have and you accept that.

You realize that what time you have is inherently uncertain and variable. In addition you'd begin to subscribe to a view of personal power, seeing that your actions are almost always a choice, and you'd accept the fact that you are making choices. This would be especially true when you choose to do something that is not immediately gratifying.

In fact, you'd accept that it is often those things which require long term focus and hard work that create the most fulfillment. So you wouldn't generally succumb to short-term hedonism and, in fact, succumb to long-range hedonism (meaning that you'd work on a longer term goals that would create better outcomes).

Chapter 17 – An Honest Mirror

What you choose to do with your time reflects your values, your self-image, what you choose to believe about time, what you believe about how long your task takes and how efficiently you complete it, and what you believe about breaks.

We have already talked about how your values are reflected in your time and what you prioritize, but did you realize that your self-image is also reflected by what you do?

A person who has a healthy self-image will tend to say, "What is the best use of my skills? What is the best use of my time-choice? Is this the best use of my skills and best programming of my schedule?"

If the answer is that it is not the best use of skills and schedule, people with a healthy self-image will find a way to change what they are doing by delegating some work to others and by selecting actions which lead to optimal productivity.

When you really start to believe that much of how you use your time may be within your power, you won't focus upon having enough or not having enough--instead, you will recognize that you are the person who controls how you will use your time, and what you do is a reflection of your values, skills, and how you view yourself. When you truly believe that not having any time is a creation of your own making, then your focus will shift from complaining to focusing upon something that you can change. You will start to take active steps to be the chooser of your tasks, the developer of your skill set, and the advocate of your abilities.

In the "mirror" below, write words which describe the actions which represent the best use of your time and skill set.

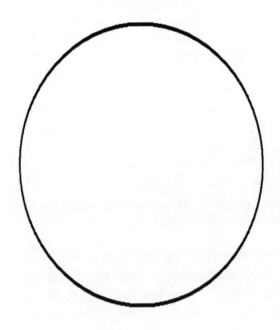

Chapter 18 – Decisiveness And Time

Being decisive is very important in terms of owning your control over your day. Certainly, you cannot control everything but there are aspects and components of choice that you have that you can exercise. Being decisive is one of these.

When you spend time waffling between choices, this is when you waste lots and lots of time. Not only that, you rob yourself of full energy for other tasks that you need to do. It is good to research and get information before you make a decision; however, this can be done in excess.

You may be thinking that you want to avoid making the wrong decision; however, how do you know if the decision is right or wrong? Don't all decisions have lessons to them and aren't these lessons of equal or greater value than any other part of the decision?

At times related to making decisions is the ability to cut your losses. When you see that things are not working out well, can you take a decisive action and stop a project from going on any further? Can you decide to fire an employee who is not working out? Or can you create a new system when you recommend that the system that you are using is not working at all?

If you have a decision that you're having a hard time making, run it through a cost-benefit analysis, and see if this helps you.

COST	BENEFIT

Chapter 19 – No Excuses and Responsibility

Whatever is not working is not working because of how you have responded to it. You have created a methodology, or a routine is in place that is continuing to operate and function, to create the exact outcome that it is set up to create.

If you don't want the outcome, then change the methods you're using. There are no excuses, no blaming, no complaining, and no whining—just stopping, stepping back and saying, "What is it about the method I use that is creating this less-than-desirable outcome? How can I revise the method and change it? Even if I cannot change it immediately, can I change it over time? If I cannot change it, how can I cut my losses?"

See if you can step back from blaming other people--even refrain from blaming yourself. See if you can step into forgiveness and now say, "What is it about the way the method is created that has created this particular outcome? What responses can I make to get the outcome that I want?"

Chapter 20 – The Role of Focus

When you decide to make a conscious effort to move in specific direction, do you stay focused? If you are able to stay focused, then you will find that you are able to complete tasks more effectively and efficiently.

Competing distractions often throw us off course. What are the distractions in your home or office? Does your phone ring nonstop? Do you respond to emails too often during the day? Are things getting lost because you fail to file? Are you out of supplies because you failed to plan ahead and order things?

Do what you can to eliminate these distractions, or at least to prevent them from getting in the way. In fact, when possible, adopt a method which will help you to ensure that these distractions will not get in your way. Then, when the time has come, you can sit and focus upon task completion.

You may initially want to procrastinate rather than focus on a task. If you find that this is coming up for you, it is probably because of a couple of things. Either you are still intending to rush and hurry and therefore you are not focusing on getting things done early and setting that as your intention, or you are holding an underlying philosophy that places a demand upon you. If so, it might be a philosophy which says that you must do things perfectly.

You begin to think about how if you don't do it perfectly others wouldn't like how you did part of it. You worry about what they might say, or about how you might get rejected. You might fantasize about the impact of not doing things as well as you would like.

If this starts to come up for you, see if you can shift your focus to the idea of what can be done *now*, simply get into action, and just take an initial step. Often, just taking this initial step will help your momentum and get you started with moving forward, and getting work done.

You may even find that you become more effective and efficient as you place no demands upon yourself. For example, when writing, I generally write a first draft of the copy in which I don't criticize or analyze any of what I have written. Is everything perfect, is there nice logical flow, does it feel conversational and easy to attend to? None of those questions are questions that I am going to evaluate in my initial work.

In fact, my focus at that point is upon completing the information, sharing something, and reminding myself that I will go back and edit *after* I have produced this initial copy.

This approach has allowed me to prevent procrastination from taking over. I reduce or eliminate the demands, and I just focus on doing the best that I can.

Even if you are not someone to plan ahead, you might find that keeping the focus of your goal in mind will help you to move toward it more easily.

Chapter 21 – Your Surroundings

Bubble gum wrappers, sneakers, and brown lunch bags lined the floor of my car. My sink was full of dishes. Laundry waited for folding in my dryer. Beach towels waited on lawn chairs for me to pick up. The dog's water bowl was empty, and the guinea pigs squeaked for alfalfa hay. It was summer and the kids were home. I could tell just by looking around.

I couldn't help but feel discouraged as I looked at my goal list for the day: exercise, shower, eat breakfast, see clients, pick up kids from camp, quality time with kids, clean house/car, edit book, prepare lecture, grade quizzes, send next ezine to subscribers, make dinner, check e-mails, thank you notes.

This was an average summer day of stuff to do, but I felt grumpy when I looked at it and realized that I wasn't going to get it all done. It seemed like there was something unremitting about my schedule & I couldn't figure out what it was. I wondered what would happen if I eliminated cleaning my house and car from the picture. I knew that this would create the time I needed.

However, I didn't like to work in a chaotic environment. What to do.

At that point, I had a choice to make.

Accept the chaos of my surroundings, or get less stuff done. However, I realized that this approach was energetically draining. As a longer-term approach, I decided that cleaning up my surroundings so as to match the efficiency I wanted was an important next step.

The most helpful thing that I did was to start by decluttering a few of my most used rooms. My goal was to go through my cluttered rooms and find 30 items to either toss or give away (from each room). Having a well defined goal made it easier and less emotional to declutter.

Rewards of the process included:
- Being able to see what was available for use
- Getting rid of things I no longer needed and donating to charity
- Being able to find what I wanted more easily
- Being able to put things away more easily
- Feeling proud of myself and unashamed of my workstation

- Noticing my mind going to "bigger" things
- Improved efficiency and productivity

Optimize your environment. It will free you to be more productive, and you'll enjoy being productive as well.

Chapter 22 – Having Fun "Making" Time

When all is said and done, you picked up this book because you wanted to "make" time—because the title told you that you didn't have "any".

You've learned that you actually do have the same amount of time as everyone else. "Making" time is a fallacy, but you can learn to start implementing action steps in a different fashion—one that reclaims your schedule.

You've learned not to buy into the stories you've been trained to tell yourself about time, but to step back and focus upon your choices.

You've clarified your values and priorities through various reflective exercises.

You've learned the value of making decisions, and you've probably even made at least one important decision while completing this book.

You've examined your ability to prioritize and follow through, despite distractions.

You've developed several plans of action, all related to various aspects of increasing efficiency.

You've started to take breaks and schedule vacations.

You've learned some efficiency tricks.

You've learned the Big 3 questions, and the secret of how to quickly eliminate blind habits which sabotage you.

You've learned about time expansion and task expansion, so that you can make choices about time which take these into consideration.

You've cleaned up your surroundings so that you can increase your efficiency.

You've probably chosen to stop whining, blaming, complaining, making excuses, or repeating things that don't work.

And I hope you've had fun in the process.

If you find that the book was a good start, but you would like to develop particular skills further, please feel free to contact me. It is my personal pleasure to coach my readers, and I would be delighted and honored to discuss this option with you.

Also, please keep in mind that I usually have at least one live event per year, so let me know if you'd like to receive the notice of this event.

Thank you for your readership.

Now, go and truly enjoy your day!

Pam Garcy, PhD
September 7, 2010

About the author

Dr. Pamela D. Garcy is a clinical psychologist and life coach who works with adults in her private practices in Dallas and Plano. Her passion is helping people to live happier and saner lives.

Pam has been interviewed as an expert and was much honored to appear on local shows in Dallas and around Texas, including *Good Morning Texas* as well as others. She has also enjoyed interviews with authors from magazines including *More, Parents, and Self.* She takes special pleasure in speaking to radio talk show hosts, including ESPN radio and others. She's also been featured in *The Dallas Morning News*, *The Oklahoman*, and *Globe and Mail.*

In addition to her clinical practice, Pam serves on the faculty of Argosy University and supervises UT Southwestern psychology interns. One of Pam's other joys is conducting intensive training workshops and conducting psycho-educational groups. She enjoys speaking on topics related to emotional health, decision making, motherhood, parenting, relationships, success-mindedness, life-balance, self-direction, and self-acceptance. When her work-hat is off, she volunteers in her children's schools.

Pam is a Cum Laude graduate of Rice University, and received graduate degrees from University of Houston and University of Texas Southwestern Medical Center. She and her husband, Dr. Roger Clifford, have been married for 21 years and are blessed with 3 lovely children, Brittany, Ethan, and Max.

It would be Pam's pleasure to discuss how she might help you or those you know.

How Pam helps people:
Individual Therapy
Group Therapy
Couples Therapy
Life Coaching
Classes
Training
Therapy Supervision
Weekend Workshops
Speaking at Your Next Event

You can contact Pam through her site at
http://www.myinnerguide.com

Or, feel free to fax this page to Pam at (972) 934-1633.

Your Name:_____

Phone:_____

E-mail:_____

Reason for Inquiry:_____

6194460R1

Made in the USA
Charleston, SC
25 September 2010